contents

British & North American Readers
Please note that Australian cup and spoon measurements are metric. A quick conversion guide appears on page 63.

drink up

Sipping on a mouth-watering frappé or smoothie will certainly complete the cafe-at-home experience. Luscious and fruity, these drinks will have you coming back for more...

fresh berry frappé

300g blueberries
250g raspberries
40 ice cubes, crushed
½ cup (125ml) fresh orange juice

Blend or process berries until just smooth. Push berry puree through fine sieve into large bowl; discard solids in sieve. Stir in ice and juice; spoon into serving glasses.

serves 4
per serving 0.3g fat; 293kJ (70 cal)

pineapple and mint frappé

1 large pineapple (2kg), peeled,
    chopped coarsely
40 ice cubes, crushed
1 tablespoon finely chopped
    fresh mint

Blend or process pineapple until smooth; transfer to large jug. Stir in ice and mint; pour into serving glasses.

serves 4
per serving 0.3g fat; 412kJ (99 cal)

banana smoothie

2 cups (500ml) milk
2 medium bananas (400g),
    chopped coarsely
½ cup (140g) yogurt
1 tablespoon honey
1 tablespoon wheat germ
¼ teaspoon ground cinnamon

Blend or process ingredients until smooth.

serves 4
per serving 6.3g fat; 776kJ (185 cal)

melon mania

600g seeded, peeled, coarsely
    chopped rockmelon
600g seeded, peeled, coarsely
    chopped honeydew melon
1kg seeded, peeled, coarsely
    chopped watermelon
250g strawberries, halved

Push fruit through a juice extractor. Stir to combine.

serves 4
per serving 1.2g fat; 625kJ (149 cal)

fresh berry frappé

banana smoothie

pineapple and mint frappé

melon mania

chicken tandoori wrap

You will need one large barbecued chicken (900g) for this recipe.

3$\frac{1}{2}$ cups (600g) chopped cooked chicken
$\frac{1}{4}$ cup (60g) tandoori paste
4 green onions, sliced
$\frac{3}{4}$ cup (200g) yogurt
2 tablespoons chopped fresh coriander
1 tablespoon lime juice
$\frac{1}{2}$ teaspoon sugar
4 pieces lavash bread
2 tablespoons mango chutney

Combine chicken, paste, onion and $\frac{1}{4}$ cup of the yogurt in heated oiled medium frying pan; cook, stirring, about 5 minutes or until hot.
Combine remaining yogurt with coriander, juice and sugar in small bowl.
Place a quarter of chicken mixture along short side of 1 piece of lavash; drizzle with a quarter of the yogurt mixture and 2 teaspoons of the chutney, roll to enclose filling. Repeat with remaining ingredients.

serves 4
per serving 18.4g fat; 2279kJ (544 cal)

chicken schnitzel burgers

4 single chicken breast
  fillets (700g)
1/4 cup (35g) plain flour
1 egg, beaten lightly
1 tablespoon milk
1/2 cup (80g) corn flake
  crumbs
1/2 cup (50g) packaged
  breadcrumbs
1 medium tomato
  (190g), seeded,
  chopped finely
1 medium avocado
  (250g), chopped finely
1 small red onion (100g),
  chopped finely
2 tablespoons
  vegetable oil
1 long loaf turkish bread
60g baby rocket leaves
sauce
1/2 cup (150g)
  mayonnaise
1 small white onion (80g),
  grated coarsely
2 tablespoons
  french dressing
1 tablespoon sweet
  fruit chutney

Using a meat mallet, gently pound chicken
between sheets of plastic wrap until 1cm thick.
Toss chicken in flour, shake away excess flour.
Dip into combined egg and milk, then in combined
crumbs to coat. Cover; refrigerate 1 hour.
Meanwhile, combine tomato, avocado and
onion in small bowl.
Heat oil in large frying pan; cook schnitzels,
in batches, until browned and cooked through.
Drain on absorbent paper; cover to keep warm.
Cut bread into four even pieces, split each piece
in half horizontally; toast cut sides lightly.
To serve, sandwich schnitzels, tomato mixture and
rocket, drizzled with the sauce, between bread.
Sauce Whisk ingredients in small bowl
until combined.

serves 4
per serving 47.1g fat; 3928kJ (938 cal)

lamb and pesto focaccia

400g lamb fillets
20cm-square piece focaccia
$\frac{1}{4}$ cup (65g) basil pesto
$\frac{1}{2}$ cup (50g) shaved parmesan cheese
$\frac{1}{4}$ cup (35g) drained sliced sun-dried tomatoes

Cook lamb on heated oiled grill plate (or grill or barbecue) until browned all over and cooked as desired. Stand lamb, covered, 5 minutes before slicing thickly.

Preheat sandwich press. Cut focaccia in half crossways, then in half horizontally. Spread pesto over bases of focaccia, top with lamb, cheese, tomato and remaining focaccia. Place focaccia in sandwich press about 5 minutes or until cheese melts and focaccia is heated through.

Slice focaccia diagonally to serve.

serves 2
per serving 32.9g fat; 3185kJ (761 cal)

char-grilled baby octopus salad

1kg baby octopus
1 clove garlic, crushed
1 teaspoon grated
  fresh ginger
2 teaspoons dry sherry
1 teaspoon brown sugar
1 teaspoon malt vinegar
½ teaspoon sesame oil
2 teaspoons kecap manis
2 teaspoons sweet
  chilli sauce
¼ cup (60ml) tomato sauce
250g cherry tomatoes,
  halved
1 small red onion (100g),
  sliced thinly
150g mesclun
2 lebanese cucumbers
  (260g), seeded,
  sliced thinly
⅓ cup coarsely chopped
  fresh coriander
dressing
¼ cup (60ml) sweet
  chilli sauce
1 tablespoon soy sauce
1 clove garlic, crushed
1 tablespoon lime juice

Remove and discard heads and beaks from octopus; cut each octopus in half.
Combine octopus in large bowl with garlic, ginger, sherry, sugar, vinegar, oil and sauces; toss to coat octopus in marinade. Cover; refrigerate 3 hours or overnight.
Just before cooking octopus, combine tomato, onion, mesclun, cucumber and coriander in large bowl.
Char-grill (or barbecue or pan-fry) undrained octopus, in batches, until browned all over and cooked through. Combine octopus with salad in bowl. Add dressing; toss gently to combine.
Dressing Combine ingredients in a screw-top jar; shake well.

serves 4
per serving 3.8g fat; 1011kJ (241 cal)

beer-battered fish and chips with tartare sauce

1½ cups (225g) self-raising flour
1 egg
1½ cups (375ml) beer
5 large potatoes (1.5kg), peeled
vegetable oil, for deep-frying
12 medium flathead fillets (660g)

tartare sauce

1 cup (300g) mayonnaise
2 teaspoons finely grated lemon rind
1 tablespoon lemon juice
2 tablespoons finely chopped gherkins
2 tablespoons drained capers, chopped finely
1 tablespoon finely chopped fresh dill
1 tablespoon finely chopped fresh chives
1 red thai chilli, seeded, chopped finely

Whisk flour, egg and beer together in medium bowl until smooth; cover, refrigerate batter 1 hour.
Cut potatoes into 1cm-wide slices; cut slices into 1cm-wide strips, dry well. Preheat oven to moderate.
Heat oil in large saucepan; deep-fry chips, in batches, until browned and cooked through. Place chips on absorbent paper on large oven tray; to keep them hot, place, uncovered, in moderate oven.
Reheat oil. Dip fish in batter; deep-fry in hot oil until browned and crisp. Serve fish and chips with tartare sauce, and lemon wedges, if desired.
Tartare sauce Combine ingredients in medium bowl; mix well.

serves 4
per serving 60.7g fat; 4952kJ (1183 cal)

kumara, chilli and coriander soup

100g fresh coriander, roots attached
1 tablespoon vegetable oil
1 large brown onion (200g), chopped coarsely
2 cloves garlic, crushed
1½ teaspoons sambal oelek
3 medium kumara (1.2kg), chopped coarsely
1 litre (4 cups) water
2 cups (500ml) chicken stock
⅔ cup (160ml) coconut milk

Wash coriander under cold running water, removing any dirt clinging to the roots; dry thoroughly. Finely chop enough of the coriander root to make 2 teaspoons; coarsely chop enough coriander leaves to make ¼ cup.

Heat oil in large saucepan; cook coriander root, onion, garlic and sambal, stirring, until onion softens. Add kumara; cook, stirring, 5 minutes. Add the water and stock; bring to a boil. Reduce heat; simmer, uncovered, about 15 minutes or until kumara softens.

Blend or process soup, in batches, until smooth; return soup to same cleaned pan. Simmer, uncovered, over medium heat until thickened slightly; add coconut milk, stir until heated through. Sprinkle coriander leaves over soup to serve.

serves 4
per serving 13.9g fat; 1483kJ (354 cal)

tip This soup can be made up to 3 days ahead and refrigerated, covered. Any leftover coriander root or leaves can be chopped, wrapped in plastic and frozen.

sumac-spiced potato wedges

Sumac is a reddish-purple ground spice made from the berries of a wild shrub grown in Lebanon. It is available from Middle-Eastern food stores and delicatessens.

5 medium potatoes (1kg)
1 egg white, beaten lightly
1 teaspoon sumac
$1/4$ teaspoon chilli powder
$1/3$ cup (110g) tomato relish

Preheat oven to very hot. Line a baking tray with baking paper.
Cut unpeeled potatoes into wedges. Combine egg white, sumac and chilli in a large bowl; add potato wedges, combine well.
Place wedges, skin-side down, on tray; bake in very hot oven for 40 minutes or until tender and golden brown. Serve with relish for dipping.

serves 4
per serving 0.4g fat; 778kJ (186 cal)

spaghetti with rocket, parmesan and pine nuts

200g spaghetti
$^{1}/_{4}$ cup (60ml) olive oil
2 cloves garlic, crushed
1 red thai chilli, chopped finely
$^{1}/_{4}$ cup (40g) roasted pine nuts
$^{1}/_{2}$ cup (40g) flaked parmesan cheese
100g baby rocket leaves

Cook pasta in large saucepan of boiling water, uncovered, until just tender; drain.
Meanwhile, heat oil in small saucepan; cook garlic and chilli, stirring, about 30 seconds or until garlic just softens and is fragrant (do not brown the garlic).
Place hot drained pasta and oil mixture in large bowl with pine nuts, cheese and rocket; toss to combine.

serves 4
per serving 24.7g fat; 1706kJ (408 cal)

mega beef burgers

1kg beef mince
1 small brown onion (80g), grated
2 cloves garlic, crushed
2 tablespoons barbecue sauce
2 tablespoons worcestershire sauce
2 teaspoons all-purpose seasoning
2 tablespoons chopped fresh flat-leaf parsley
½ cup (35g) stale breadcrumbs
1 egg, beaten lightly
2 large brown onions (400g), extra, sliced
12 rindless bacon rashers, halved
6 eggs, extra
6 hamburger buns
75g mesclun

Combine beef in large bowl with grated onion,
garlic, sauces, seasoning, parsley, breadcrumbs
and egg; shape mixture into 6 patties.
Cook patties in oiled large non-stick frying pan
(or on barbecue plate) until browned both sides
and cooked through. Cook sliced onion, bacon
and extra eggs in same pan until onion is soft,
bacon crisp and eggs cooked as desired.
Split buns; toast both sides. Sandwich mesclun,
burgers, onion, bacon and eggs between buns.

serves 6
per serving 30.7g fat; 2883kJ (689 cal)

chicken caesar salad

You will need one large barbecued chicken (900g)
for this recipe.

100g parmesan cheese
1 egg
1 clove garlic, quartered
2 tablespoons lemon juice
$^{1}/_{2}$ teaspoon dijon mustard
10 anchovy fillets, drained
$^{3}/_{4}$ cup (180ml) olive oil
1 large cos lettuce, torn
$3^{1}/_{2}$ cups (600g) coarsely chopped, cooked chicken
170g packet croutons

Using a vegetable peeler, slice cheese
into thin ribbons.
Blend or process egg, garlic, juice,
mustard and half of the anchovy until smooth.
With motor operating, add oil in a thin, steady
stream; process until dressing just thickens.
Just before serving, combine cheese in large
bowl with lettuce, chicken, croutons and remaining
anchovy; toss gently to combine. Drizzle with
anchovy dressing to serve.

serves 4
per serving 80.6g fat; 4306kJ (1029 cal)
tip The dressing can be made a day ahead
and refrigerated, covered.

bruschetta caprese

$^1/_2$ x long loaf turkish bread
50g baby rocket leaves
250g cherry tomatoes, sliced thickly
100g bocconcini cheese, sliced thickly
2 tablespoons finely shredded fresh basil
2 tablespoons olive oil

Cut turkish bread crossways into four even pieces. Split each piece in half horizontally; toast both sides.
Top each piece of turkish bread with equal amounts of rocket, tomato, cheese and basil; drizzle with oil to serve.

serves 4
per serving 15.1g fat; 1463kJ (350 cal)

thai beef salad

500g beef fillet
3 medium green cucumbers (510g),
   peeled, sliced thickly
4 red thai chillies, sliced thinly
3 green onions, sliced thinly
$1/2$ cup loosely packed fresh mint leaves
$1/2$ cup loosely packed fresh coriander leaves
lemon grass dressing
1 clove garlic, crushed
2 teaspoons finely chopped fresh lemon grass
2 teaspoons finely chopped fresh coriander root
1 tablespoon lime juice
2 tablespoons light soy sauce
$1/2$ teaspoon fish sauce
2 teaspoons brown sugar

Cook beef on heated oiled grill plate (or grill
or barbecue) until browned all over and cooked
as desired. Stand 5 minutes; slice thinly.
Place beef, cucumber, chilli, onion, herbs
and lemon grass dressing in large bowl;
toss gently to combine.
Lemon grass dressing Combine ingredients
in small bowl.

serves 4
per serving 6.2g fat; 798kJ (191 cal)

prawn laksa

1kg medium uncooked prawns
1/3 cup (90g) laksa paste
2 1/4 cups (560ml) coconut milk
1.25 litres (5 cups) chicken stock
2 red thai chillies, seeded, chopped finely
1/4 cup (60ml) lime juice
1 tablespoon brown sugar
6 fresh vietnamese mint leaves, torn
250g dried rice noodles
vegetable oil, for shallow-frying
300g fresh firm tofu, cut into 2cm cubes
2 1/2 cups (200g) bean sprouts
2 green onions, chopped finely

Shell and devein prawns, leaving tails intact.
Heat large dry saucepan; cook paste, stirring, until fragrant. Stir in milk, stock, chilli, juice, sugar and mint. Bring to a boil; simmer, covered, 30 minutes.
Meanwhile, cook noodles in large saucepan of boiling water, uncovered, until just tender; drain.
Heat oil in wok or large heavy-based frying pan; cook tofu, in batches, until browned all over. Drain on absorbent paper.
Add prawns to laksa mixture; simmer, uncovered, about 5 minutes or until prawns are just changed in colour.
Just before serving, add noodles, tofu, sprouts and onion to pan; stir gently until ingredients are combined and laksa is hot.

serves 4
per serving 49.9g fat; 3581kJ (856 cal)
tip Substitute regular mint for vietnamese mint, if preferred.

zucchini and pumpkin frittata

500g butternut pumpkin, peeled,
   chopped coarsely
2 large zucchini (300g), chopped coarsely
1 tablespoon olive oil
200g fetta, crumbled
8 eggs
1/2 cup (125ml) cream

Preheat oven to moderately hot. Oil and line
base and side of deep 22cm-round cake pan
with baking paper.
Combine pumpkin and zucchini, in single layer,
in large baking dish; drizzle with oil. Roast, uncovered,
in moderately hot oven about 30 minutes or until
vegetables are browned and tender.
Reduce oven temperature to moderately slow.
Place pumpkin, zucchini and fetta in prepared pan.
Whisk eggs in medium bowl until frothy. Whisk
in cream; pour over vegetables and fetta. Bake,
uncovered, in moderately slow oven, about
40 minutes or until frittata sets and is just cooked
through. Serve with a rocket and pine nut salad,
drizzled with balsamic dressing, if desired.

serves 4
per serving 41g fat; 2101kJ (502 cal)

choose your brew...

These informative pages will increase your knowledge of the many ways to serve the world's favourite beverage: coffee.

Ways to drink coffee…

Espresso Also known as short black. An espresso is a shot (30ml) of pure bliss. It should have a thick golden "crema" on the surface, proving the espresso was brewed correctly. Espresso is the basis for most other coffee beverages.

Cappuccino Equal parts espresso, steamed milk and milk froth, sprinkled with chocolate powder.

Espresso con panna An espresso topped with whipped cream, sprinkled with chocolate powder.

Flat white An espresso topped with steamed milk (no froth).

Long black Also known as espresso lungo. An espresso diluted with hot water to make the drink longer and slightly weaker.

Ristretto Means "restricted" in Italian. An extremely short espresso, made with less water, making it even darker, stronger and more concentrated than an espresso.

Doppio Not for the faint-hearted, this is a double shot of espresso and tends to be very strong.

Macchiato An espresso "stained" with a tiny amount of hot, cold or frothed milk.

Caffe latte Simply coffee with milk. One-quarter espresso and three-quarters steamed milk. The milk and coffee blend, leaving a layer of foamed milk on top.

Latte macchiato An espresso poured into a tall glass of hot, frothed milk; the coffee "marks" or creates a marbling pattern in the thick froth.

Mocha Also known as mochaccino. An equal blend of espresso and hot drinking chocolate topped with frothed milk.

For the perfect cup…

- Always use freshly roasted coffee that has been correctly ground.
- Use filtered water.
- Remember "less is more". Don't allow too much water to pass through the coffee grounds – about 30ml for a true espresso.
- Coffee should not be brewed at boiling point – the high temperature releases a bitter element into the brew.

How to froth milk…

- Make sure the milk is straight from the fridge.
- Skim, light and soy milk are all suitable to steam.
- A stainless steel jug able to hold two cups of milk is best.
- Don't overheat the milk while steaming. If the jug becomes too hot to touch, you have boiled the milk. Boiled milk will not aerate.
- For a creamy cappuccino, lightly tap the jug base a few times on the bench after steaming; let stand for a moment to reduce the large bubbles.
- Practice steaming milk – it's a skill that may not come to you immediately, but a little persistence will pay off in the shape of perfect froth.
- Wipe the steam arm with a clean, damp cloth between each use. This removes any built-up milk.

mixed mushroom risotto

*Arborio is a small, wide-grained, pearly rice variety
which is ideal for making risotto as it readily absorbs
stock without becoming mushy.*

10g dried porcini mushrooms
1 cup (250ml) boiling water
1 litre (4 cups) chicken stock
1$\frac{1}{2}$ cups (375ml) water
40g butter
2 tablespoons olive oil
2 medium brown onions (300g), chopped finely
200g cup mushrooms, sliced thinly
2 cups (400g) arborio rice
1 cup (80g) finely grated parmesan cheese

Place porcini mushrooms in medium heatproof
bowl, cover with the boiling water; stand 30 minutes.
Drain mushrooms, reserving $\frac{1}{2}$ cup (125ml) of liquid.
Bring reserved liquid, stock and the water to a boil
in medium saucepan; reduce heat, cover, keep hot.
Heat butter and oil in large saucepan; cook onion
and all mushrooms, stirring, until onion is soft.
Add rice; stir to coat in oil mixture. Stir in 1 cup
of the stock mixture; cook over low heat, stirring,
until liquid is absorbed.
Continue adding stock mixture, in 1-cup batches,
stirring, until absorbed after each addition. Total
cooking time should be about 35 minutes or
until rice is just tender. Stir in cheese to serve.

serves 4
per serving 26.7g fat; 2820kJ (674 cal)

eggplant and artichoke pasta

1 medium eggplant (300g)
1 tablespoon cooking salt
200g bucatini
¼ cup (60ml) olive oil
1 tablespoon olive oil, extra
1 medium brown onion
  (150g), sliced thinly
2 cloves garlic, crushed
3 medium tomatoes (570g),
  chopped coarsely
100g button mushrooms,
  halved
1 small red capsicum
  (150g), sliced thinly
2 tablespoons tomato paste
400g can artichoke hearts,
  drained, quartered
1 cup (125g) frozen peas,
  thawed, drained
1 tablespoon chopped
  fresh basil
1 tablespoon chopped
  fresh oregano
⅔ cup (50g) grated
  parmesan cheese

Cut unpeeled eggplant into 1cm slices; place in colander. Sprinkle all over with salt; stand 30 minutes.

Meanwhile, cook pasta, uncovered, in large saucepan of boiling water until just tender; drain.

Rinse eggplant well under cold running water; pat dry with absorbent paper. Heat oil in large frying pan; cook eggplant, in batches, until browned both sides. Drain eggplant on absorbent paper. Discard any remaining oil in pan; wipe pan clean with absorbent paper.

Heat extra oil in same cleaned pan; cook onion and garlic, stirring, until onion softens. Add tomato, mushroom, capsicum and tomato paste; cook, stirring, until vegetables are just tender. Add artichoke, peas and herbs; cook, stirring occasionally, until mixture is heated through.

Add pasta and eggplant; toss gently until hot. Serve immediately, sprinkled with cheese.

serves 4
per serving 23.8g fat; 1992kJ (476 cal)

roasted tomato, goat cheese and chicken pizza

500g cherry tomatoes, halved
2 tablespoons balsamic vinegar
2 tablespoons brown sugar
2 chicken breast fillets (340g)
25cm pizza base
2 tablespoons chopped fresh coriander
80g goat cheese
40g baby rocket leaves

Preheat oven to very hot.
Place tomato on oven tray lined with baking paper, drizzle with combined vinegar and sugar; cook, uncovered, in very hot oven about 25 minutes or until tomato is soft.
Meanwhile, cook chicken on heated oiled grill plate (or in frying pan) until browned both sides and cooked through. Cool 5 minutes, cut into thin slices.
Reduce oven temperature to hot. Place pizza base on oven tray; cook in hot oven about 10 minutes or until lightly browned.
Increase oven temperature to very hot. Top pizza with tomato, chicken, coriander and crumbled cheese. Bake in very hot oven, uncovered, 10 minutes or until pizza is browned and crisp. Serve topped with rocket.

serves 2
per serving 20.4g fat; 3029kJ (724 cal)

bean nachos

Mexican-style beans are a mildly spiced,
canned combination of red kidney or pinto beans,
capsicum and tomato.

420g can mexican-style beans, drained
290g can red kidney beans, rinsed, drained, mashed
2 tablespoons tomato paste
1 tablespoon water
230g packet plain corn chips
1½ cups (185g) coarsely grated cheddar cheese
1 large avocado (320g)
1 small red onion (100g), chopped finely
1 large tomato (250g), chopped finely
1 teaspoon lemon juice
½ cup (120g) sour cream
1 tablespoon coarsely chopped fresh coriander

Preheat oven to moderately hot. Heat combined
beans, paste and the water, stirring, in large
non-stick frying pan. Cover; keep warm.
Place corn chips in large ovenproof dish;
sprinkle with cheese. Bake in moderately hot
oven 5 minutes or until cheese melts.
Meanwhile, mash avocado in small bowl; stir in
half of the combined onion and tomato, and juice.
Top heated corn chips with bean mixture, avocado
mixture and sour cream; sprinkle nachos with
remaining onion and tomato, and coriander.

serves 4
per serving 60g fat; 3840kJ (917 cal)

hokkien noodle stir-fry

500g hokkien noodles
1 tablespoon peanut oil
1 teaspoon sesame oil
500g beef fillet, sliced thinly
1 medium brown onion (150g), sliced thickly
1 clove garlic, crushed
2 teaspoons grated fresh ginger
1 medium red capsicum (200g), sliced thinly
1 medium green capsicum (200g), sliced thinly
2 tablespoons lemon juice
2 tablespoons sweet chilli sauce
1 tablespoon sesame seeds, toasted
1 tablespoon chopped fresh coriander
1 tablespoon chopped fresh mint

Rinse noodles under hot water; drain. Transfer
to large bowl; separate noodles with fork.
Heat both oils in wok or large frying pan;
stir-fry beef, in batches, until browned all over.
Add onion, garlic and ginger to wok; stir-fry until
onion softens. Add capsicums; stir-fry until just
tender. Return beef to wok with noodles, juice and
sauce; stir-fry until hot. Stir in seeds and herbs.

serves 4
per serving 14.1g fat; 1770kJ (423 cal)

tip Place beef in the freezer for about 1 hour
before using, to make it easier to slice.

roasted capsicum, goat cheese and walnut pasta salad

375g large spiral pasta
2 medium red capsicums (400g)
2 medium yellow capsicums (400g)
150g goat cheese, crumbled
$1/3$ cup (35g) walnuts, toasted, chopped coarsely
$1/2$ cup loosely packed fresh basil leaves
$1/4$ cup (60ml) red wine vinegar
$1/3$ cup (80ml) olive oil
1 clove garlic, crushed
2 teaspoons wholegrain mustard

Cook pasta in large saucepan of boiling water, uncovered, until just tender; drain. Rinse under cold water; drain.
Meanwhile, quarter capsicums, remove and discard seeds and membranes. Roast under grill or in very hot oven, skin-side up, until skin blisters and blackens. Cover capsicum pieces with plastic or paper for 5 minutes, peel away skin; slice capsicum thickly.
Place pasta and capsicum in large bowl with cheese, walnuts, basil and combined remaining ingredients; toss gently to combine.

serves 4
per serving 31.6g fat; 2727kJ (651 cal)

tip Fetta or any soft, crumbly cheese can be used instead of the goat cheese, and toasted pecan halves make a nice change from walnuts.

friands

Friands are rich and buttery, and very easy to make.
These can be made up to four days ahead.

185g butter, melted
1 cup (110g) almond or hazelnut meal
6 egg whites, beaten lightly
1½ cups (240g) icing sugar mixture
½ cup (75g) plain flour

Preheat oven to moderately hot. Grease
12 oval or rectangular friand moulds or a
12-hole muffin pan (⅓ cup/80ml).
Combine butter, almond or hazelnut meal,
egg white, sifted icing sugar and flour in a
large bowl; stir until combined.
Divide mixture among prepared pan/s; bake in
moderately hot oven about 30 minutes or until
browned. Turn friands onto wire rack to cool.
variations
banana Slice 1 small banana (260g); place banana
slices on top of mixture in pan/s just before baking.
chocolate hazelnut Scatter 50g of chopped milk
chocolate over the mixture and press a halved
hazelnut on top of each friand before baking.
berry Scatter 75g of blueberries, raspberries,
mulberries or blackberries over the mixture just
before baking.

makes 12
per friand 17.8g fat; 1137kJ (272 cal)
banana 17.8g fat; 1188kJ (284 cal)
chocolate hazelnut 19.1g fat; 1235kJ (295 cal)
berry 17.8g fat; 1142kJ (273 cal)

banana bread

You will need 1 large overripe banana for this recipe.

1¼ cups (185g) self-raising flour
1 teaspoon ground cinnamon
20g butter
½ cup (100g) firmly packed brown sugar
1 egg, beaten lightly
¼ cup (60ml) milk
½ cup mashed banana

Preheat oven to hot. Grease 14cm x 21cm loaf pan, line base with baking paper.
Sift flour and cinnamon into large bowl, rub in butter. Stir in sugar, egg, milk and banana. Do not over-mix; the batter should be lumpy.
Spoon mixture into prepared pan; bake in hot oven about 30 minutes or until cooked when tested. Stand bread 10 minutes before turning onto wire rack to cool.

makes 12 slices
per slice 2.2g fat; 474kJ (113 cal)

tip To serve, toast banana bread and top with cream cheese and honey, if desired.

summer berry almond tart

1²/₃ cups (250g) plain flour
¹/₃ cup (55g) icing
    sugar mixture
2 teaspoons grated
    orange rind
150g cold butter, chopped
1 egg
350g fresh mixed berries
    (strawberries, blueberries,
    raspberries, blackberries
    or mulberries)
almond filling
90g butter, softened
¹/₂ teaspoon vanilla essence
¹/₂ cup (110g) caster sugar
1 egg
1 tablespoon plain flour
1 cup (100g) almond meal

Process flour, icing sugar, rind and butter until combined. Add egg, process until pastry just comes together. Shape pastry into a round; cover and refrigerate 1 hour.

Roll pastry between two sheets of baking paper until large enough to line base and side of 26cm (top measurement) loose-base flan tin. Ease pastry into tin, press lightly into the side; trim edges with a sharp knife or rolling pin. Place the tin on an oven tray and refrigerate 15 minutes.

Preheat oven to moderate. Cover pastry with baking paper; fill with dried beans or rice. Bake in moderate oven 10 minutes. Remove paper and beans, bake further 5 minutes or until pastry is golden brown; cool.

Spoon almond filling into pastry case. Scatter berries over almond filling. Bake in moderate oven about 35 minutes or until filling is golden brown and firm to touch; cool. Serve dusted with sifted icing sugar, if desired.

Almond filling Beat butter, essence and sugar in small bowl with electric mixer until pale. Beat in egg until combined. Stir in flour and almond.

serves 8
per serving 33.3g fat; 2144kJ (512 cal)

sticky date pudding with butterscotch sauce

1¼ cups (200g) seeded dried dates
1¼ cups (310ml) boiling water
1 teaspoon bicarbonate of soda
50g butter, chopped
½ cup (100g) firmly packed brown sugar
2 eggs, beaten lightly
1 cup (150g) self-raising flour
butterscotch sauce
¾ cup (150g) firmly packed brown sugar
300ml cream
80g butter, chopped

Preheat oven to moderate. Grease deep
20cm-round cake pan; line base with baking paper.
Combine dates and the water in medium heatproof
bowl. Stir in soda; stand 5 minutes.
Blend or process date mixture with butter and
sugar until pureed. Add eggs and flour; process
until just combined. Pour mixture into prepared pan.
Bake, uncovered, in moderate oven about 1 hour
(cover with foil if pudding starts to overbrown).
Stand 10 minutes; turn onto serving plate.
Serve warm with butterscotch sauce.
Butterscotch sauce Combine ingredients
in medium saucepan; stir over low heat until
sauce is smooth and slightly thickened.

serves 8
per serving 41.3g fat; 2974kJ (710 cal)

tiramisu cake

6 eggs
1 cup (220g) caster sugar
1 cup (150g) self-raising
   flour
1/2 cup (75g) cornflour
1 cup (250ml) boiling water
1 1/2 tablespoons dry
   instant coffee
1/2 cup (125ml) marsala
1/4 cup (25g) finely grated
   dark chocolate
300ml thickened
   cream, whipped
75g dark chocolate, extra
mascarpone filling
4 egg yolks
1/3 cup (75g) caster sugar
1/4 cup (60ml) marsala
2 cups (500g) mascarpone

Preheat oven to moderate. Grease two 19cm-square cake pans, line bases with baking paper.

Beat eggs and sugar in large bowl with electric mixer for about 8 minutes or until thick and creamy. Gently fold in triple-sifted flours alternately with 1/4 cup (60ml) of the boiling water. Divide mixture evenly between prepared pans and bake in moderate oven 25 minutes. Stand sponges 5 minutes before turning onto wire racks to cool.

Combine remaining boiling water, coffee and marsala in small bowl; cool.

Line a clean 19cm-square cake pan with plastic wrap; split each sponge cake in half. Place one layer of cake in the base of pan; brush 1/3 cup (80ml) of coffee mixture over cake, spread with 1 cup of mascarpone filling, sprinkle with 1 tablespoon of grated chocolate.

Repeat layers, ending with a cake layer; cover, refrigerate 3 hours or overnight.

Turn cake onto serving plate, spread top and sides with whipped cream. Using a vegetable peeler, make chocolate curls from extra dark chocolate and sprinkle over cake.

Mascarpone filling Beat egg yolks and sugar in small bowl with electric mixer until thick and creamy. Add marsala and mascarpone; beat until just combined.

serves 12
per serving 40.2g fat; 2604kJ (622 cal)

tip This recipe can be made two days ahead; store, covered, in the refrigerator.

lime syrup coconut muffins

2½ cups (375g) self-raising flour
1 cup (90g) desiccated coconut
1 cup (220g) caster sugar
1 tablespoon finely grated lime rind
1 cup (250ml) buttermilk
125g butter, melted
2 eggs
lime syrup
½ cup (110g) caster sugar
¼ cup (60ml) water
2 teaspoons finely grated lime rind
⅓ cup (80ml) lime juice

Preheat oven to moderately hot. Grease
12-hole (⅓ cup/80ml) muffin pan.
Combine flour, coconut and sugar in large bowl;
stir in combined remaining ingredients. Spoon
mixture into prepared pan; bake in moderately
hot oven about 20 minutes.
Transfer muffins to wire rack over tray; pour
hot lime syrup over hot muffins. Drain syrup
from tray and pour over muffins again.
Lime syrup Combine ingredients in small
saucepan; stir over heat, without boiling,
until sugar dissolves. Simmer, uncovered,
without stirring, 2 minutes.

makes 12
per muffin 15.1g fat; 1506kJ (360 cal)

hazelnut biscotti

1⅓ cups (200g) plain flour
⅓ cup (50g) self-raising flour
1 cup (220g) caster sugar
2 eggs, beaten lightly
½ cup (75g) roasted hazelnuts
1 teaspoon vanilla essence

Preheat oven to moderate.
Sift flours and sugar into large bowl. Add egg,
nuts and essence; stir until mixture becomes
a firm dough. Knead on lightly floured surface
until mixture just comes together; shape mixture
into 25cm log.
Place on greased oven tray; bake in moderate
oven about 35 minutes or until firm, cool on tray.
Using a serrated or electric knife, cut log into
5mm diagonal slices. Place slices on ungreased
oven trays; bake in moderate oven about
10 minutes or until biscotti are dry and crisp.

makes 25 slices
per slice 2.4g fat; 390kJ (93 cal)

tip To roast hazelnuts, spread nuts on oven tray;
roast in moderate oven about 5 minutes or until nuts
are golden brown (stir nuts once during roasting).
Wrap nuts in tea-towel; rub vigorously to remove
most of the skin.

glossary

all-purpose seasoning available from supermarkets; packaged combination of herbs and spices, including paprika, onion, salt and pepper.

almond meal also known as ground almond.

arborio rice small, round-grain rice well-suited to absorb a large amount of liquid.

bacon rashers also known as slices of bacon; made from smoked, cured pork.

bicarbonate of soda also known as baking soda.

breadcrumbs
  corn flake crumbs: corn flakes crushed into crumbs.
  packaged: fine-textured, crunchy, purchased, white breadcrumbs.
  stale: one- or two-day-old bread crumbed by grating, blending or processing.

bucatini a type of pasta; resembles tubular spaghetti.

butter use salted or unsalted (sweet) butter; 125g is equal to one stick of butter.

buttermilk sold alongside fresh milk in supermarkets; despite implication of name, is low in fat. Commercially made similarly to yogurt.

capers grey-green buds of a warm-climate shrub, sold either dried and salted or pickled in a vinegar brine.

capsicum also known as bell pepper or, simply, pepper. They can be red, green, yellow, orange or purplish black.

cheese
  bocconcini: delicate, semi-soft white cheese. Spoils rapidly so must be kept in refrigerator, in brine, for two days at most.

cheddar: semi-hard cow-milk cheese. It ranges in colour from white to pale-yellow and has a slightly crumbly texture.

fetta: a crumbly textured goat- or sheep-milk cheese with a sharp, salty taste.

goat: made from goat milk; has an earthy, strong taste.

mascarpone: cultured cream product; whitish to creamy-yellow in colour, with a soft, creamy texture.

parmesan: also known as parmigiano, parmesan is a hard, grainy cow-milk cheese. The curd is salted in brine for a month then aged for up to two years in humid conditions.

chilli
  powder: the Asian variety is the hottest, made from ground chillies; substitute ½ teaspoon ground chilli powder per 1 medium chopped fresh chilli.
  red thai: small, hot chillies; bright-red to dark-green in colour.
  sweet chilli sauce: mild sauce made from red chillies, sugar, garlic and vinegar.

coconut milk the second pressing from grated mature coconut flesh; available in cans and cartons.

cornflour also known as cornstarch.

cos lettuce also known as roma lettuce; has crisp, elongated leaves.

cream, thickened (minimum fat content 35%) a whipping cream containing a thickener.

dried rice noodles also known as rice stick noodles; made from rice flour and water, available wide or very thin.

eggplant also known as aubergine.

fish sauce also called nam pla or nuoc nam; made from pulverised salted fermented fish, most often anchovies. Has a pungent smell and strong taste; use sparingly.

flour
  plain: all-purpose wheat flour.
  self-raising: plain flour sifted with baking powder in the proportion of 1 cup flour to 2 teaspoons baking powder.

focaccia flat Italian-style bread.

ginger, fresh also known as green or root ginger.

herbs we have specified when to use fresh or dried herbs. We used dried (not ground) herbs in the proportion of 1:4 for fresh herbs, for example, 1 teaspoon dried herbs instead of 4 teaspoons (1 tablespoon) chopped fresh herbs.

hokkien noodles also known as stir-fry noodles. Fresh wheat-flour noodles; resemble thick, yellow-brown spaghetti.

kecap manis Indonesian thick soy sauce which has sugar and spices added.

kumara orange-fleshed sweet potato.

lavash bread flat, unleavened bread of Mediterranean origin.

lebanese cucumber long, slender and thin-skinned; this variety also known as the European or burpless cucumber.

lemon grass a tall, clumping, lemon-smelling and -tasting, sharp-edged grass; the white lower part of each stem is chopped and used in cooking.

marsala a sweet fortified wine originally from Sicily.

mayonnaise we used whole-egg mayonnaise.

mesclun a salad mix or gourmet salad mix with an assortment of young lettuce and other green leaves.

mince meat also known as ground meat, as in beef, pork, lamb and veal.

mushrooms, dried porcini rich-flavoured mushrooms; rarely found fresh. Use small amount due to strong flavour.

oil
olive: made from ripened olives. Extra virgin and virgin are the best; extra light or light refers to taste not fat levels.
peanut: pressed from ground peanuts; has high smoke point.
sesame: made from roasted, crushed white sesame seeds. Do not use for frying.

onion
green: also known as scallion or (incorrectly) shallot; immature onion picked before the bulb has formed, having a long, bright-green edible stalk.
red: also known as spanish, red spanish or bermuda onion; sweet, large, purple-red onion.

pine nuts also known as pignoli.

prawns also known as shrimp.

pumpkin also known as squash.

rocket also known as arugula, rugula and rucola; a peppery-tasting green leaf which can be used similarly to baby spinach leaves. Baby rocket leaves are both smaller and less peppery.

sambal oelek (also ulek or olek) a salty paste made from ground chillies and vinegar.

sour cream we used a thick, commercially cultured, soured cream.

soy sauce sauce made from fermented soy beans. Several variations are available in most supermarkets and Asian food stores.

sprouts tender new growths of assorted beans and seeds germinated for consumption in salads and stir-fries.

stock available in cans or tetra packs. Stock cubes or powder can be used. As a guide, 1 teaspoon of stock powder or 1 small crumbled stock cube mixed with 1 cup (250ml) water will give a fairly strong stock.

sugar we used coarse, granulated table sugar, also known as crystal sugar, unless otherwise specified.
brown: an extremely soft, fine granulated sugar retaining molasses for its characteristic colour and flavour.
caster: also known as superfine or finely granulated table sugar.
icing sugar mixture: also known as confectioners' sugar or powdered sugar; granulated sugar crushed together with a small amount of cornflour added.

sumac a purple-red astringent spice ground from the berries of a variety of Mediterranean shrub. Available in Middle-Eastern food stores and some delicatessens.

tofu also known as bean curd; an off-white, custard-like product made from the "milk" of crushed soy beans. Available fresh, as soft or firm.

tomato
paste: triple-concentrated tomato puree used to flavour soups, stews, sauces and casseroles.
sauce: also known as tomato ketchup.
canned: whole peeled tomatoes in natural juices.
egg: also called plum or roma, these are smallish, oval-shaped tomatoes.
cherry: also known as Tiny Tim or Tom Thumb tomatoes; small and round.
sun-dried: dehydrated tomatoes; we used sun-dried tomatoes that were packaged in oil, unless specified otherwise.

turkish bread also known as pide; comes in long (about 45cm) flat loaves as well as individual rounds; made from wheat flour.

vanilla essence also known as vanilla extract.

vietnamese mint narrow-leafed pungent herb; also known as laksa leaf or daun laksa.

wheatgerm small creamy flakes milled from the embryo of the wheat.

zucchini also known as courgette.

index

facts & figures

These conversions are approximate only, but the difference between an exact and the approximate conversion of various liquid and dry measures is minimal and will not affect your cooking results.

Measuring equipment

The difference between one country's measuring cups and another's is, at most, within a 2 or 3 teaspoon variance. (For the record, 1 Australian metric measuring cup holds approximately 250ml.) The most accurate way of measuring dry ingredients is to weigh them. For liquids, use a clear glass or plastic jug having metric markings.

Note: NZ, Canada, USA and UK all use 15ml tablespoons. Australian tablespoons measure 20ml. All cup and spoon measurements are level.

How to measure

When using graduated measuring cups, shake dry ingredients loosely into the appropriate cup. Do not tap the cup on a bench or tightly pack the ingredients unless directed to do so. Level the top of measuring cups and measuring spoons with a knife. When measuring liquids, place a clear glass or plastic jug having metric markings on a flat surface to check accuracy at eye level.

Dry measures

metric	imperial
15g	1/2oz
30g	1oz
60g	2oz
90g	3oz
125g	4oz (¼lb)
155g	5oz
185g	6oz
220g	7oz
250g	8oz (½lb)
280g	9oz
315g	10oz
345g	11oz
375g	12oz (¾lb)
410g	13oz
440g	14oz
470g	15oz
500g	16oz (1lb)
750g	24oz (1½lb)
1kg	32oz (2lb)

We use large eggs having an average weight of 60g.

Liquid measures

metric	imperial
30 ml	1 fluid oz
60 ml	2 fluid oz
100 ml	3 fluid oz
125 ml	4 fluid oz
150 ml	5 fluid oz (¼ pint/1 gill)
190 ml	6 fluid oz
250 ml (1cup)	8 fluid oz
300 ml	10 fluid oz (½ pint)
500 ml	16 fluid oz
600 ml	20 fluid oz (1 pint)
1000 ml (1litre)	1¾ pints

Helpful measures

metric	imperial
3mm	⅛in
6mm	¼in
1cm	½in
2cm	¾in
2.5cm	1in
6cm	2½in
8cm	3in
20cm	8in
23cm	9in
25cm	10in
30cm	12in (1ft)

Oven temperatures

These oven temperatures are only a guide. Always check the manufacturer's manual.

	°C (Celsius)	°F (Fahrenheit)	Gas Mark
Very slow	120	250	1
Slow	150	300	2
Moderately slow	160	325	3
Moderate	180 –190	350 – 375	4
Moderately hot	200 – 210	400 – 425	5
Hot	220 – 230	450 – 475	6
Very hot	240 – 250	500 – 525	7

at your fingertips

These elegant slipcovers store up to 10 mini books and make the books instantly accessible.

And the metric measuring cups and spoons make following our recipes a piece of cake.

Book Holder
Australia and overseas:
$8.95 (incl. GST).

Metric Measuring Set
Australia: $6.50 (incl. GST).
New Zealand: $A8.00.
Elsewhere: $A9.95.
Prices include postage and handling. This offer is available in all countries.

Mail or fax Photocopy and complete the coupon below and post to
ACP Books Reader Offer,
ACP Publishing, GPO Box 4967,
Sydney NSW 2001, *or* fax to (02) 9267 4967.

Phone Have your credit card details ready, then phone 136 116 (Mon-Fri, 8.00am-6.00pm; Sat, 8.00am-6.00pm).

Australian residents We accept the credit cards listed on the coupon, money orders and cheques.
Overseas residents We accept the credit cards listed on the coupon, drafts in $A drawn on an Australian bank, and also British, New Zealand and U.S. cheques in the currency of the country of issue. Credit card charges are at the exchange rate current at the time of payment.

Photocopy and complete coupon below

- -

☐ **Book Holder**　☐ **Metric Measuring Set**
Please indicate number(s) required.

Mr/Mrs/Ms _____

Address _____

_____

Postcode _____ Country _____

Ph: Business hours ( ) _____

I enclose my cheque/money order for $ _____ payable to ACP Publishing.

OR: please charge $ _____ to my ☐ Bankcard ☐ Mastercard

☐ Visa ☐ American Express ☐ Diners Club

Expiry date ____ /____

Card number

Cardholder's signature _____

Please allow up to 30 days delivery within Australia.
Allow up to 6 weeks for overseas deliveries.
Both offers expire 31/12/03. HLMCF03

Food director Pamela Clark
Food editor Louise Patniotis
ACP BOOKS STAFF
Editorial director Susan Tomnay
Creative director Hieu Chi Nguyen
Senior editor Julie Collard
Designer Mary Keep
Publishing manager (sales) Jennifer McDonald
Publishing manager (rights & new projects) Jane Hazell
Brand manager Donna Gianniotis
Pre-press Harry Palmer
Production manager Carol Currie
Publisher Sue Wannan
Group publisher Jill Baker
Chief executive officer John Alexander
Produced by ACP Books, Sydney.
Printing by Dai Nippon Printing in Hong Kong.
Published by ACP Publishing Pty Limited, 54 Park St, Sydney; GPO Box 4088, Sydney, NSW 1028. Ph: (02) 9282 8618 Fax: (02) 9267 9438.
acpbooks@acp.com.au
www.acpbooks.com.au
To order books phone 136 116.
Send recipe enquiries to
Recipeenquiries@acp.com.au
Australia Distributed by Network Services, GPO Box 4088, Sydney, NSW 1028. Ph: (02) 9282 8777 Fax: (02) 9264 3278.
United Kingdom Distributed by Australian Consolidated Press (UK), Moulton Park Business Centre, Red House Road, Moulton Park, Northampton, NN3 6AQ. Ph: (01604) 497 531 Fax: (01604) 497 533 acpukltd@aol.com
Canada Distributed by Whitecap Books Ltd, 351 Lynn Ave, North Vancouver, BC, V7J 2C4, Ph: (604) 980 9852 Fax: (604) 980 8197 customerservice@whitecap.ca
www.whitecap.ca
New Zealand Distributed by Netlink Distribution Company, Level 4, 23 Hargreaves St, College Hill, Auckland 1, Ph: (9) 302 7616.

Clark, Pamela.
Cafe food.

Includes index.
ISBN 1 86396 296 4

1. Snack foods. 2. Cookery.
I. Title. II. Title: Cafe food.
III. Title: Australian Women's Weekly.

641.53

Cover: Lamb and pesto focaccia, page 8.
Stylist: Kate Brown
Photographer: Stuart Scott
Home economist for photography: Jeanette Schembri
Back cover: on right, Chicken tandoori wrap, page 4.

The publishers would like to thank Bison Homewares and Citizen Cane Interiors for props used in photography.